CW01379240

CAN I SEE SANTA AT THE NORTH POLE?

Geography Lessons for 3rd Grade
Children's Explore the World Books

BABY PROFESSOR
EDUCATION KIDS

Speedy Publishing LLC

40 E. Main St. #1156

Newark, DE 19711

www.speedypublishing.com

Copyright 2017

All Rights reserved. No part of this book may be reproduced or used in any way or form or by any means whether electronic or mechanical, this means that you cannot record or photocopy any material ideas or tips that are provided in this book.

In stories, Santa Claus has his workshop at the North Pole. Is it really there? Can you visit it? Let's find out!

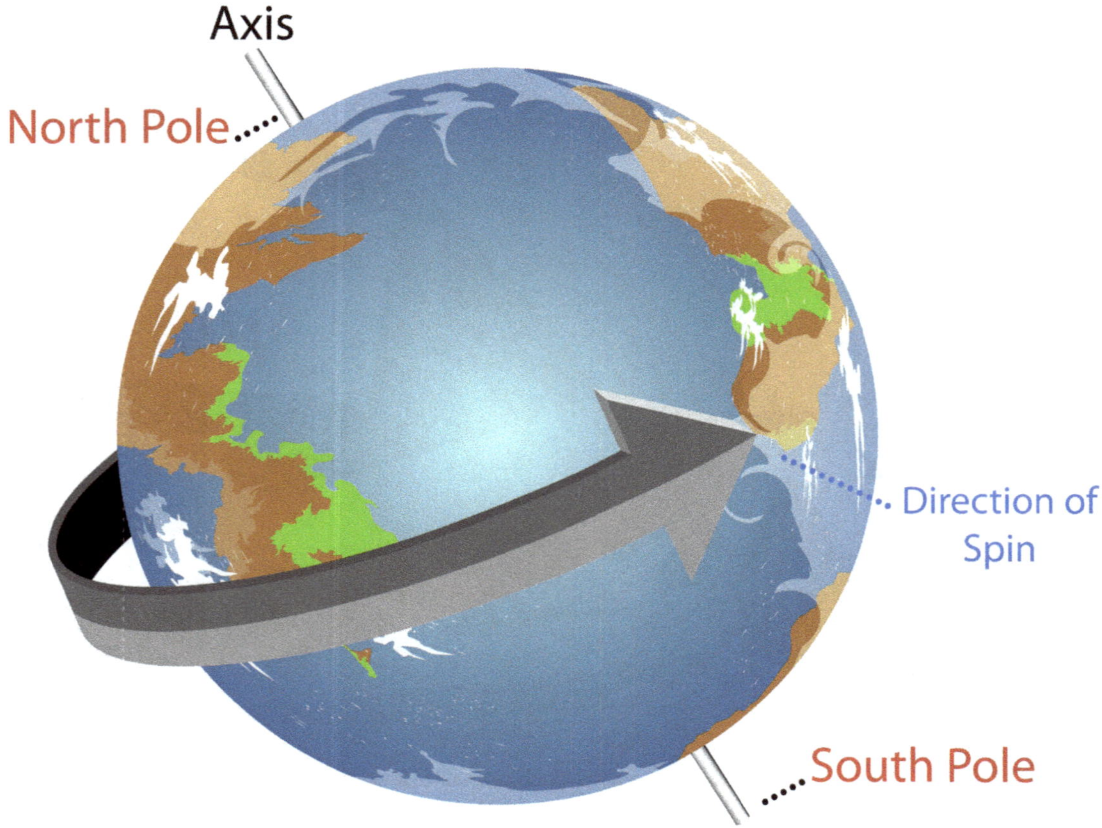
Axis
North Pole
Direction of
Spin
South Pole

THERE'S NO POLE AT THE NORTH POLE!

The North Pole is not a physical thing, like a flag pole or a telephone pole. It's real, but it's not visible.

The Earth rotates once every twenty-four hours on its axis. The axis is not a visible thing: it's just a line through the Earth around which the planet spins. The North and South Poles are the opposite ends of that axis.

If you look at a map, you may see horizontal and vertical lines. These are called lines of latitude and longitude, they are marked in degrees, and they help to measure where things are on the Earth. The longitude lines run parallel to the axis of the Earth, and they all draw together at the North and South poles.

TEACHER AND CHILDREN LOOKING AT GLOBE

EQUATOR LINE

The latitude lines start with zero degrees at the equator and climb to 90 degrees at each pole.

When you are at the North Pole, at 90 degrees North latitude, wherever you look, you are looking south! It's the top of the world!

CLIMATE

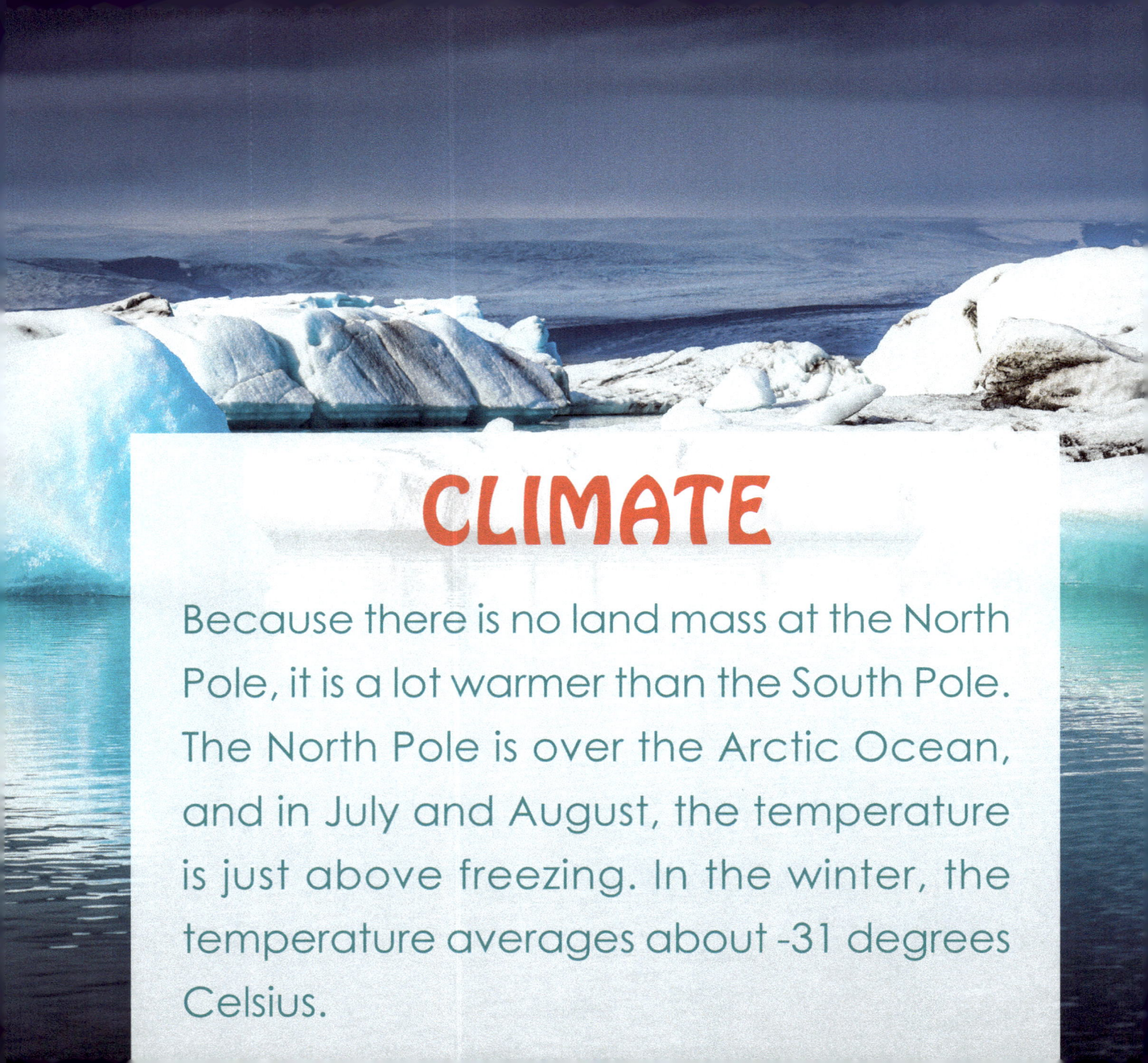

Because there is no land mass at the North Pole, it is a lot warmer than the South Pole. The North Pole is over the Arctic Ocean, and in July and August, the temperature is just above freezing. In the winter, the temperature averages about -31 degrees Celsius.

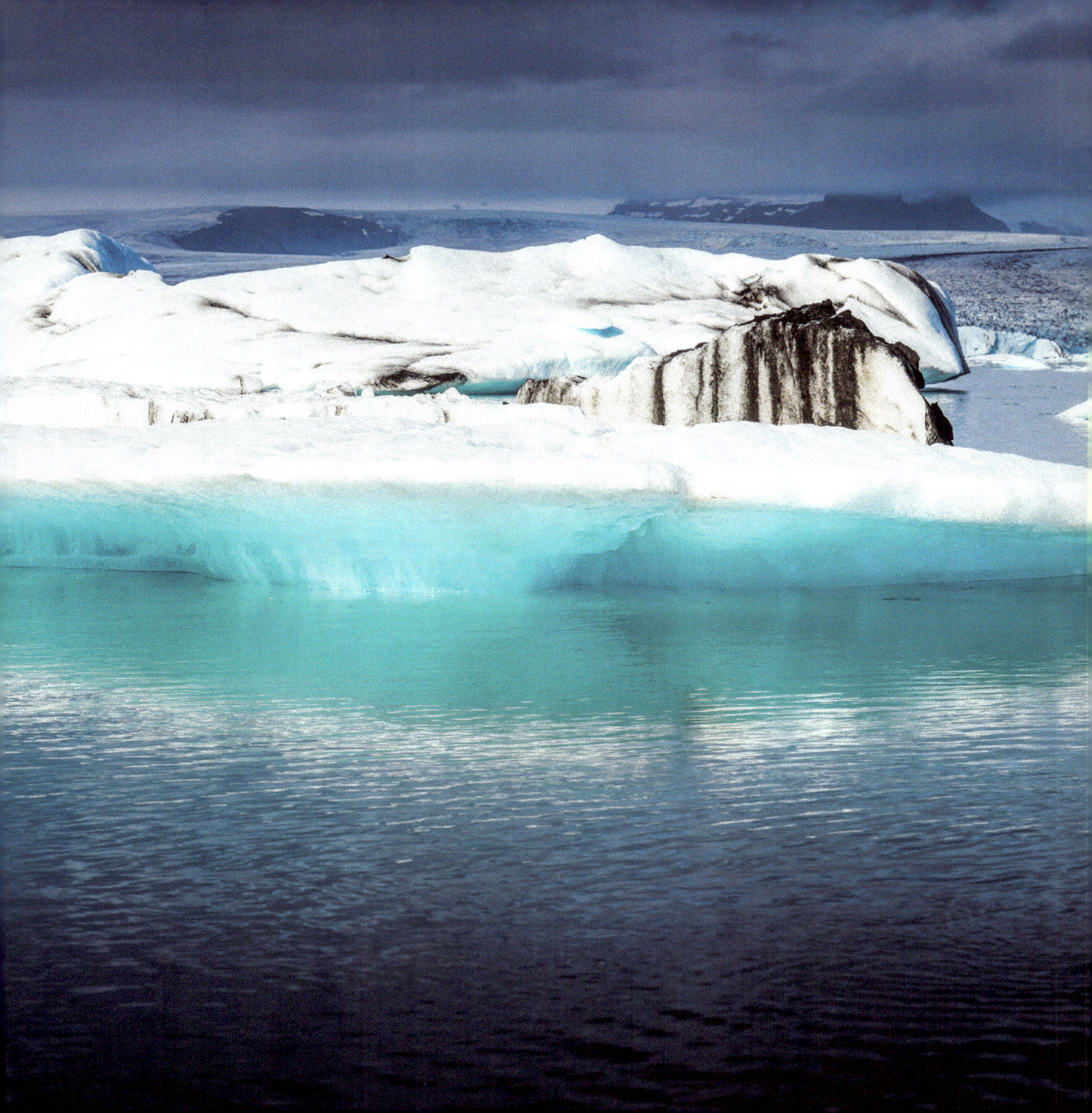

ICEBERG IN ARCTIC OCEAN

At the North Pole there is normally a sheet of ice about 8 feet thick, although its thickness varies. As global warming is causing climate change, the Arctic ice pack is getting less and less reliable, and we will see coming summers when there is no ice at all at the North Pole. Learn more about climate change in the Baby Professor books *Mother Earth Needs a Band-aid!* and *What Every Child Should Know about Climate Change.*

GEOGRAPHY

The North Pole is in the middle of the Arctic Ocean, so there are no hills, valleys, or rivers to learn about. There is also no permanent place for people to live at the North Pole. The Soviet Union, and now Russia, has maintained floating research stations near the North Pole, and scientists have worked in them for a few months each year.

RESEARCH STATION IN THE ARCTIC

At the Pole, the Arctic Ocean is about four thousand meters deep. The nearest land is the northern coast of Greenland, about 700 kilometers away. The nearest place to the North Pole where people live year-round is Alert, in northern Canada, about 820 kilometers from the Pole.

TASIILAQ, GREENLAND

DAY, NIGHT, AND TIME

Because the axis of the Earth is a little tilted in relation to the Sun, in the summer there are more hours of daylight and in the winter there are more hours of darkness. This is taken to an extreme at the North Pole!

South magnetic pole

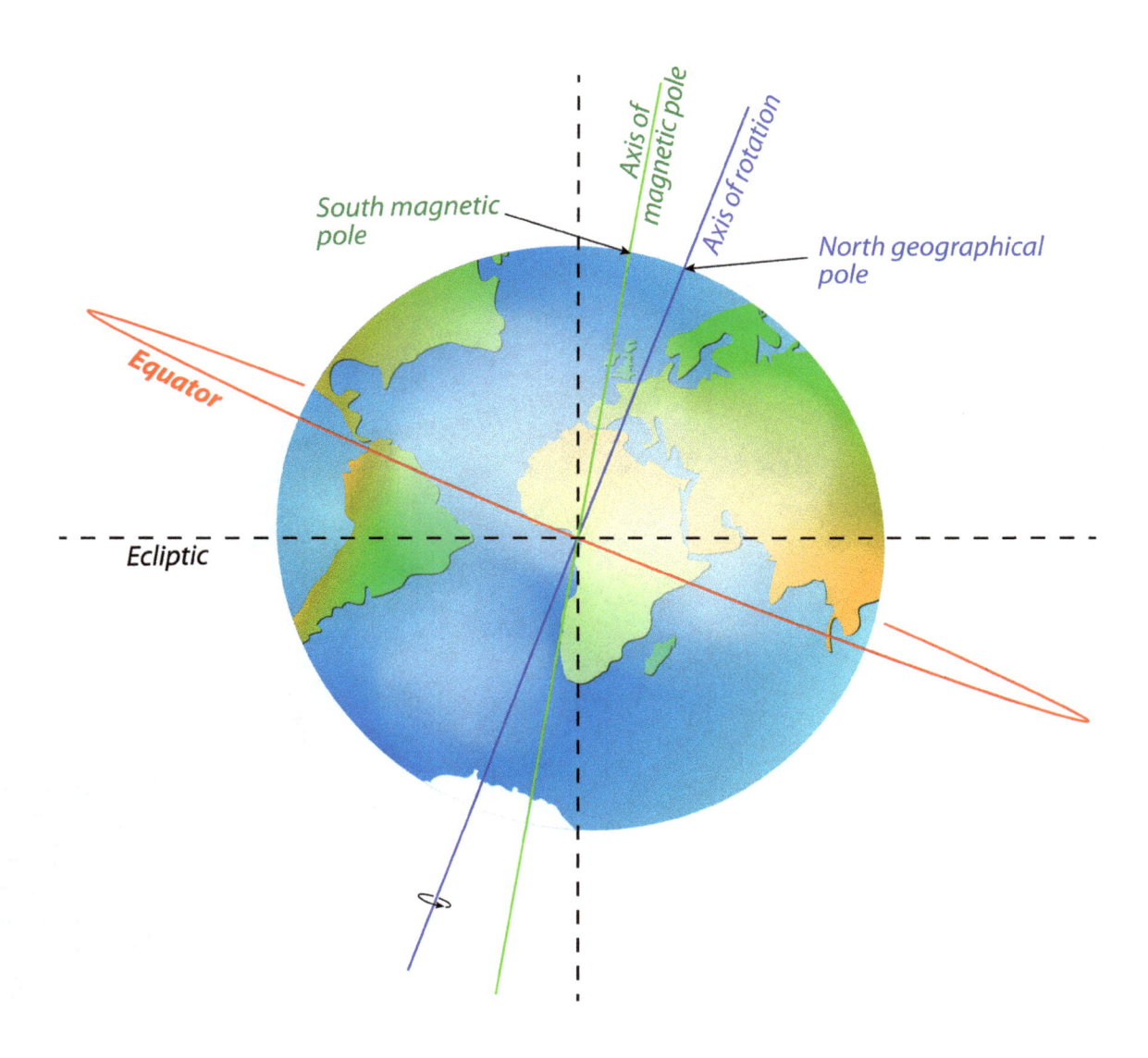

Axis of magnetic pole

Axis of rotation

North geographical pole

Equator

Ecliptic

AXIAL TILT OF THE EARTH

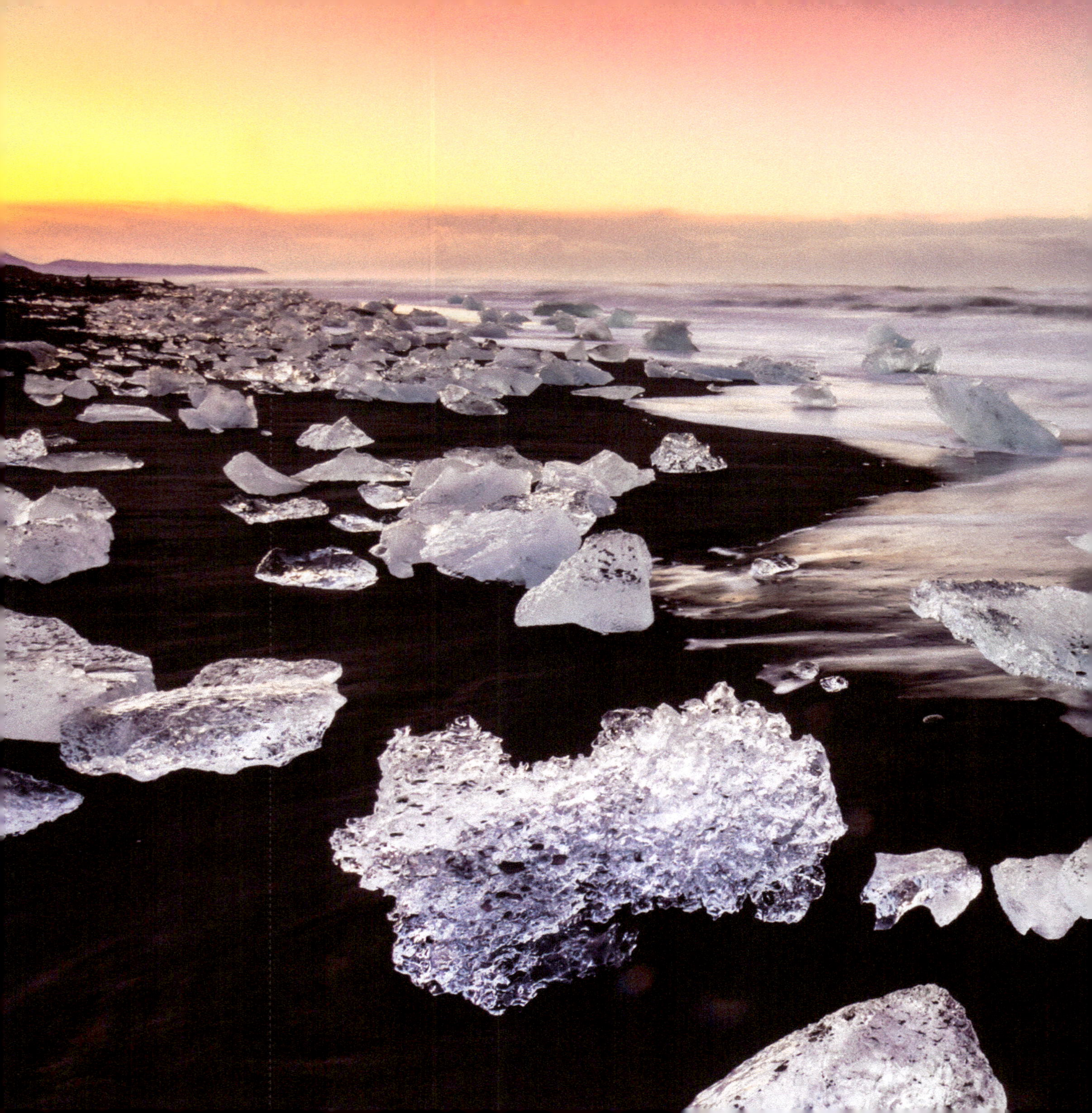

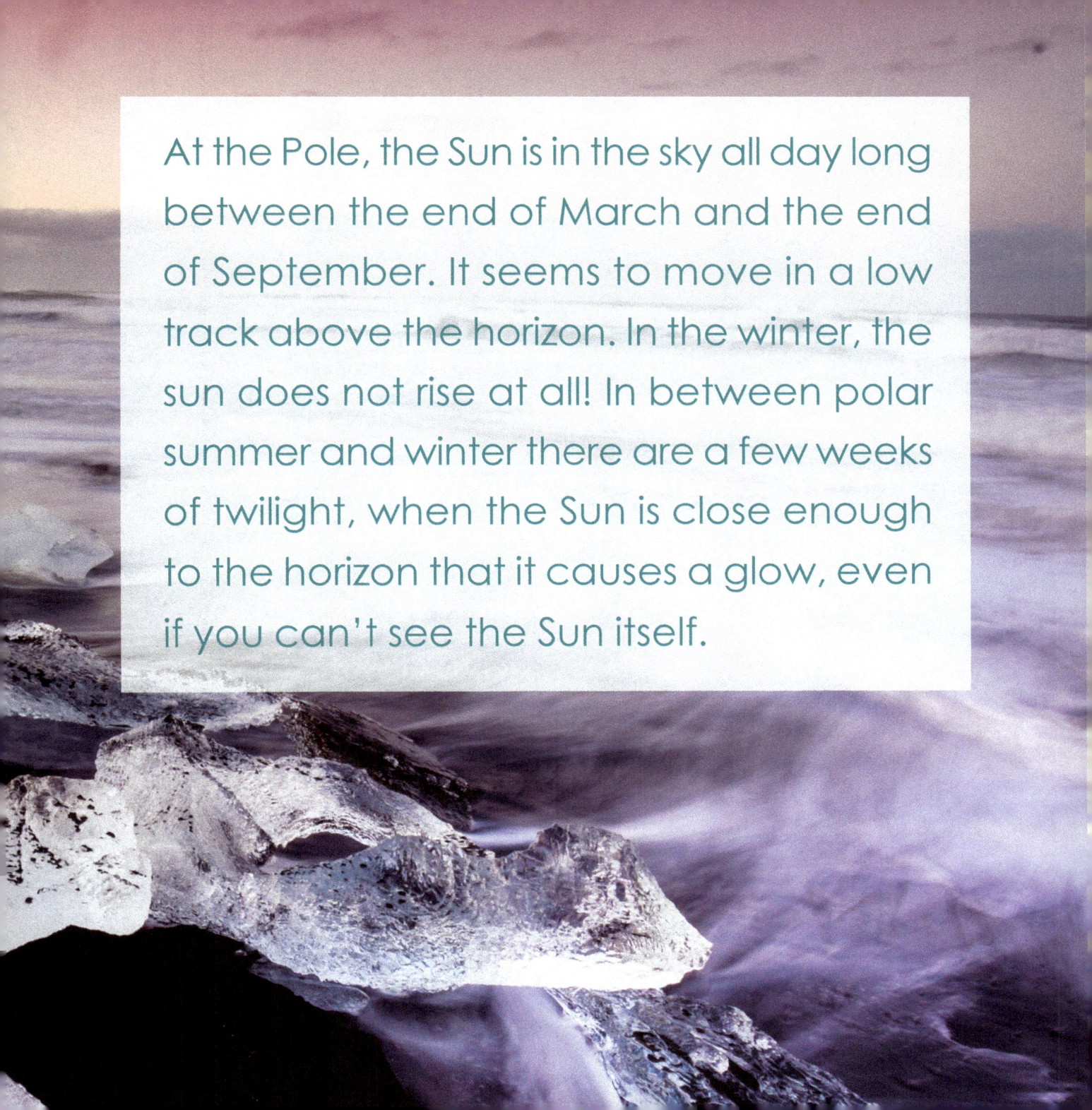

At the Pole, the Sun is in the sky all day long between the end of March and the end of September. It seems to move in a low track above the horizon. In the winter, the sun does not rise at all! In between polar summer and winter there are a few weeks of twilight, when the Sun is close enough to the horizon that it causes a glow, even if you can't see the Sun itself.

Anybody living near the North Pole has to get used to days and nights that have little or no relationship to how much light is in the sky.

Time can be a little tricky, too. All around the Earth we have a system of time zones, so that, in each zone, the Sun will be highest in the sky around noon each day. When it is noon in London, for instance, it is either 8 am or 9 am in New York City, depending on whether Daylight Saving Time is in force.

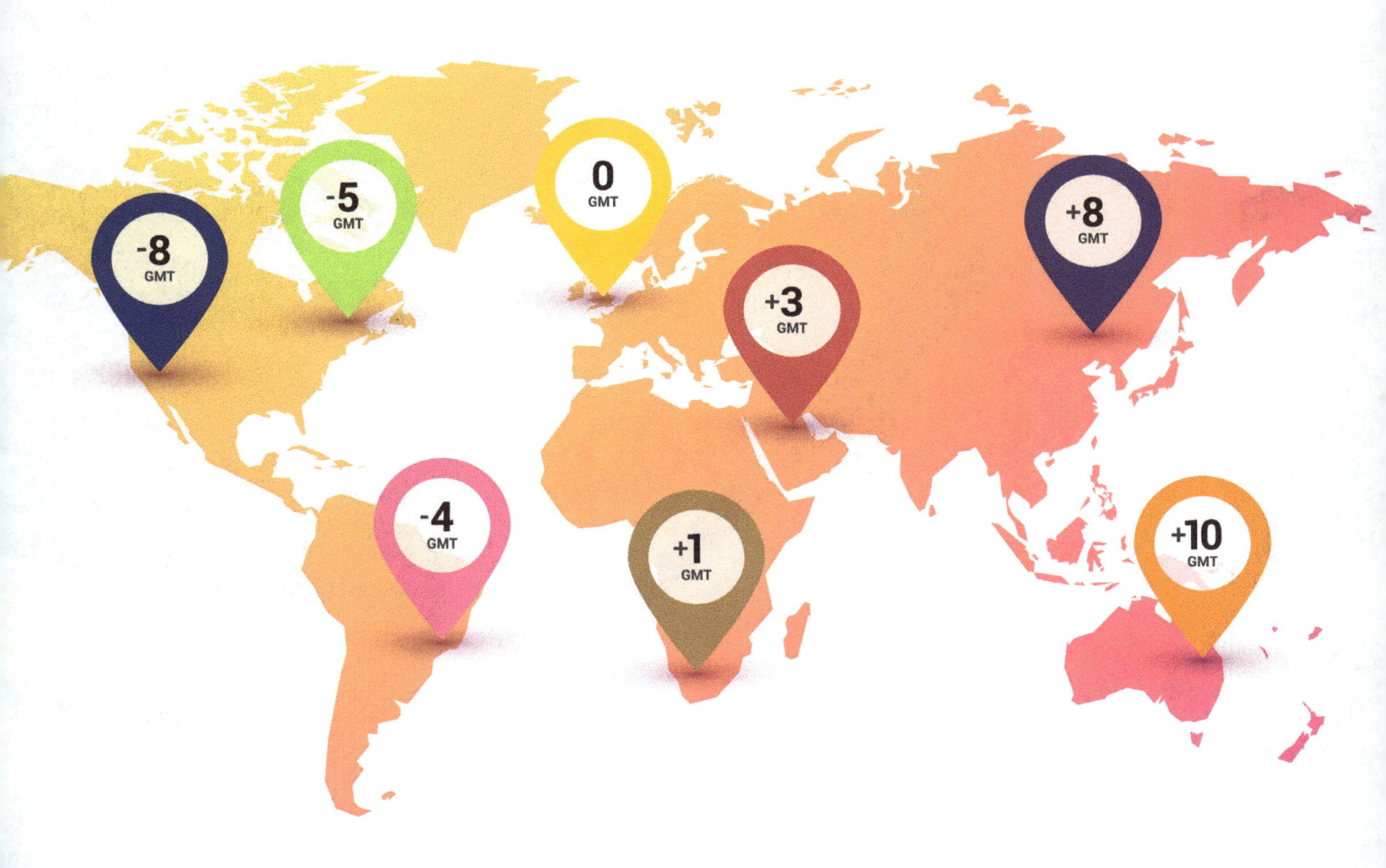

TIME ZONES WORLD MAP

AIRPORT CLOCK

But all the time zones of the whole world converge at the North and South Poles. That means that, if you were at the Pole, the time of day would be any hour you wanted it to be. This makes things a little confusing for record-keeping, but in practice people who visit the North Pole tend to use the time zone of the town or settlement they last left on their way north.

FIRST TO THE POLE!

For hundreds of years, European explorers tried to find a way to reach the North Pole. They assumed there was no land, but the spirit of curiosity and adventure drove them on. They also hoped to learn if there was a passage that ships could take from Europe to Asia and back again.

ICE BREAKER SHIP IN ICEBERG FILLED WATER

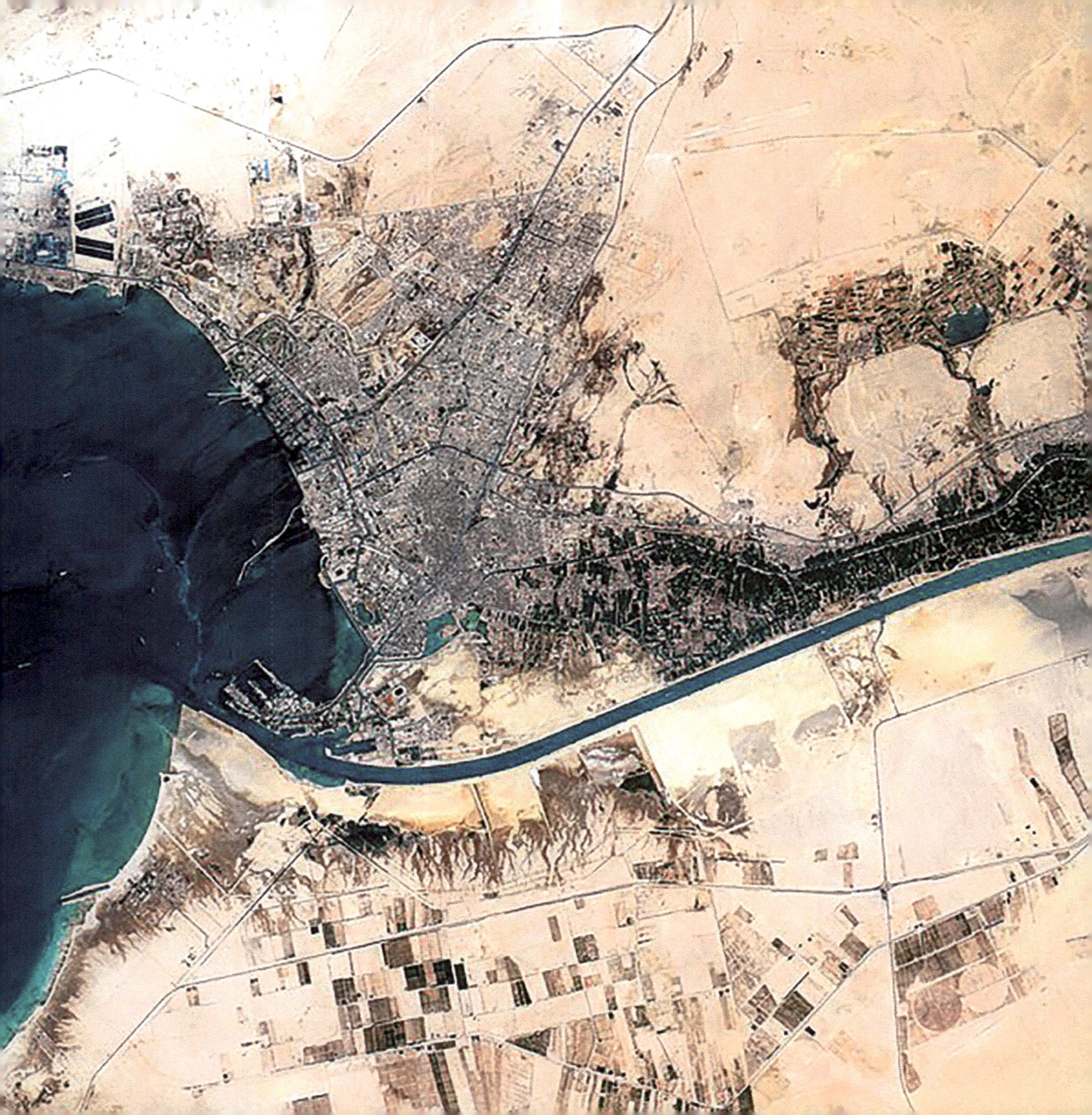

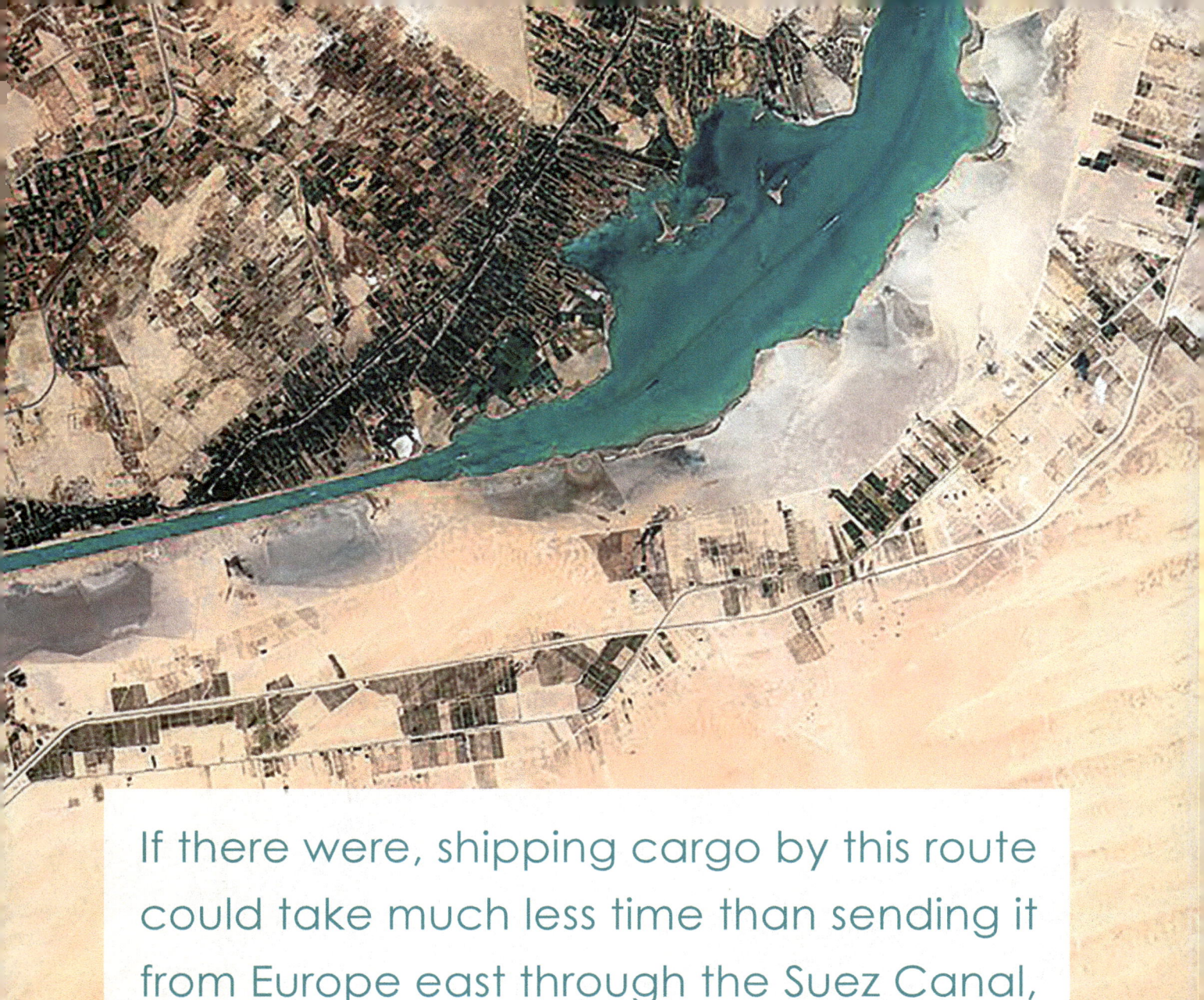

If there were, shipping cargo by this route could take much less time than sending it from Europe east through the Suez Canal, or south around Africa.

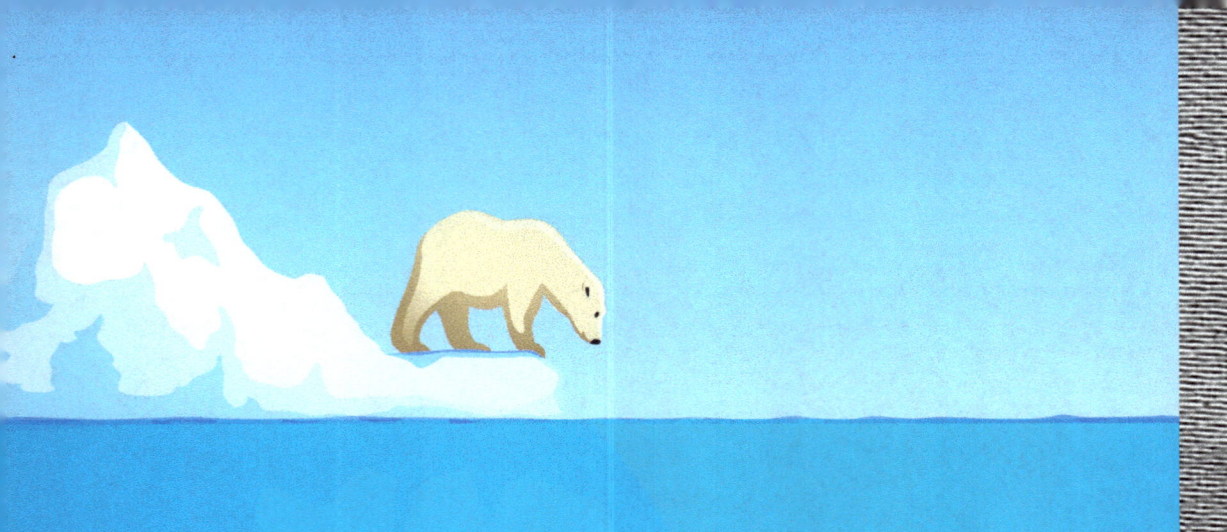

In 1871, the Parry Expedition got as far as 82 degrees north latitude. Other expeditions failed, sometimes with great loss of life. In 1881, half of an expedition team died when pack ice crushed their ship, the USS *Jeanette*.

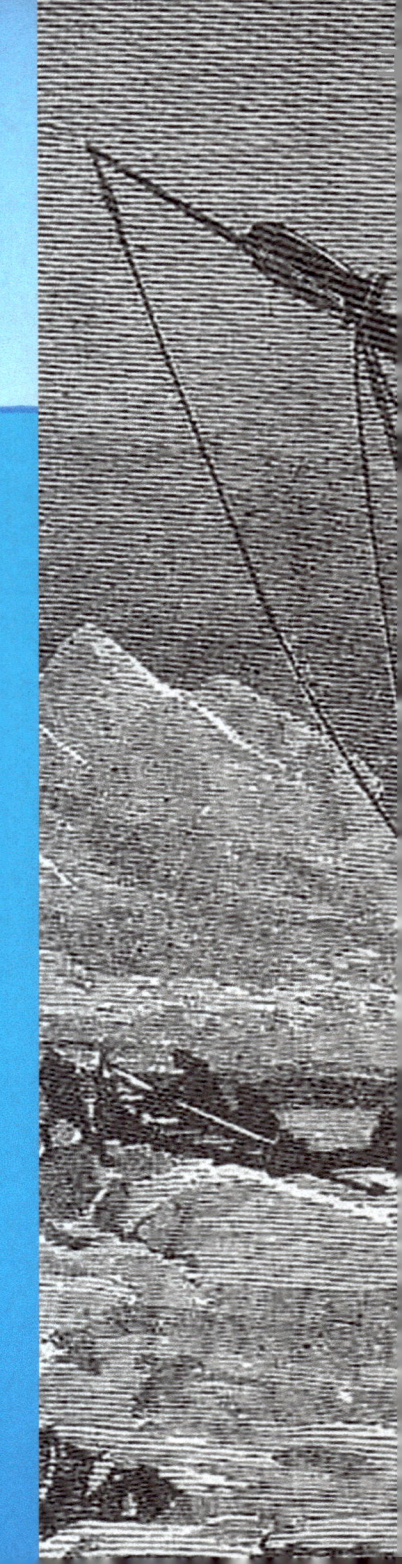

JEANNETTE SINKING

THE 1897 DISASTER

In 1895, a Norwegian expedition made it as far as 86 degrees north latitude before they had to turn back. In 1897 some Swedes tried to travel to the North Pole using a hydrogen balloon. They did not succeed, and died on Kvitøya, an Arctic island.

Frederick Cook of the U.S. claimed to reach the North Pole in 1908, but could not prove his claim. The claim by Robert Peary and his expedition in 1909 was also disputed.

Finally, in 1926, Norwegian Roald Amundsen and Lincoln Ellsworth of the United States used an airship to fly from Norway to Alaska over the North Pole.

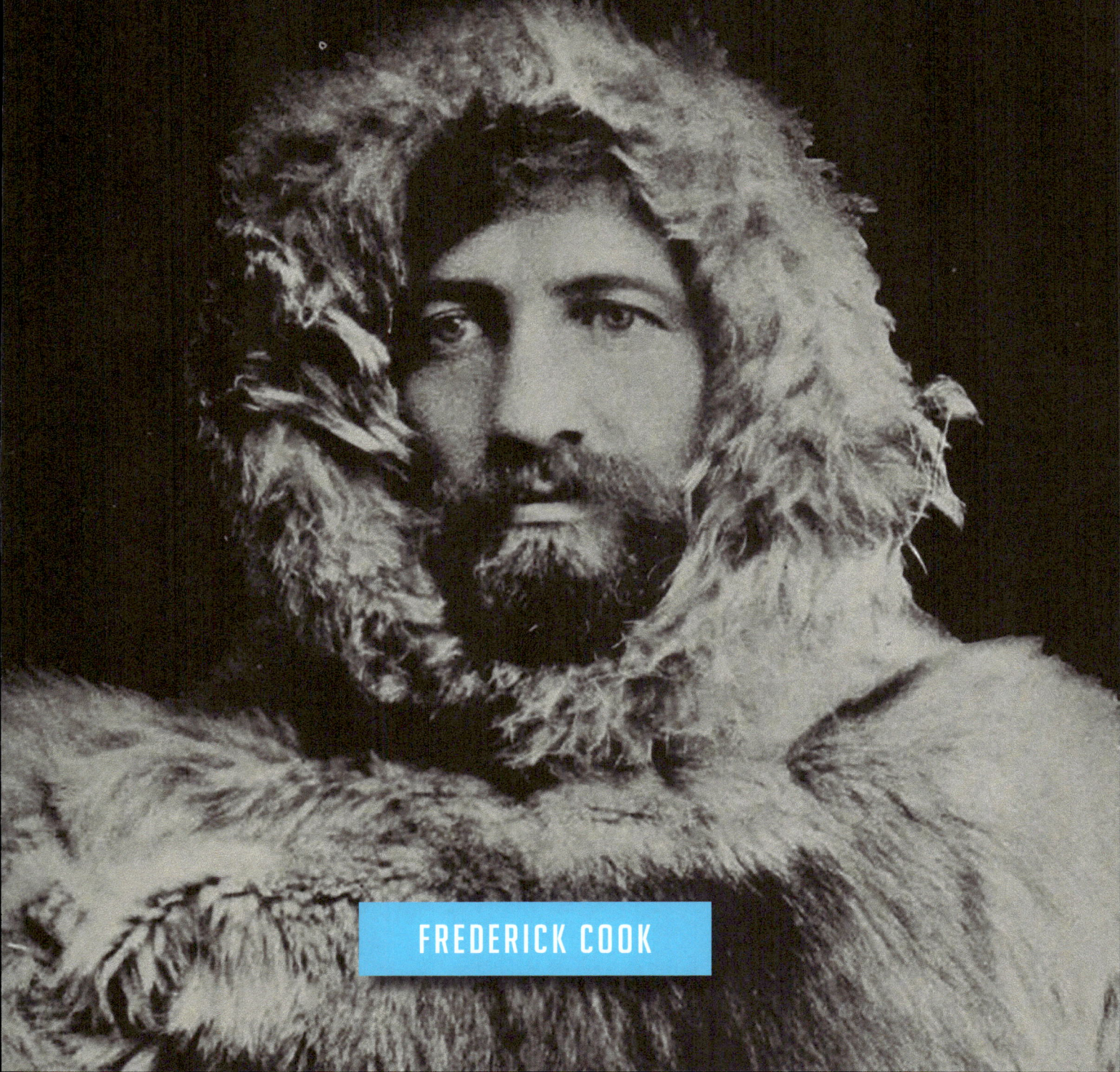

FREDERICK COOK

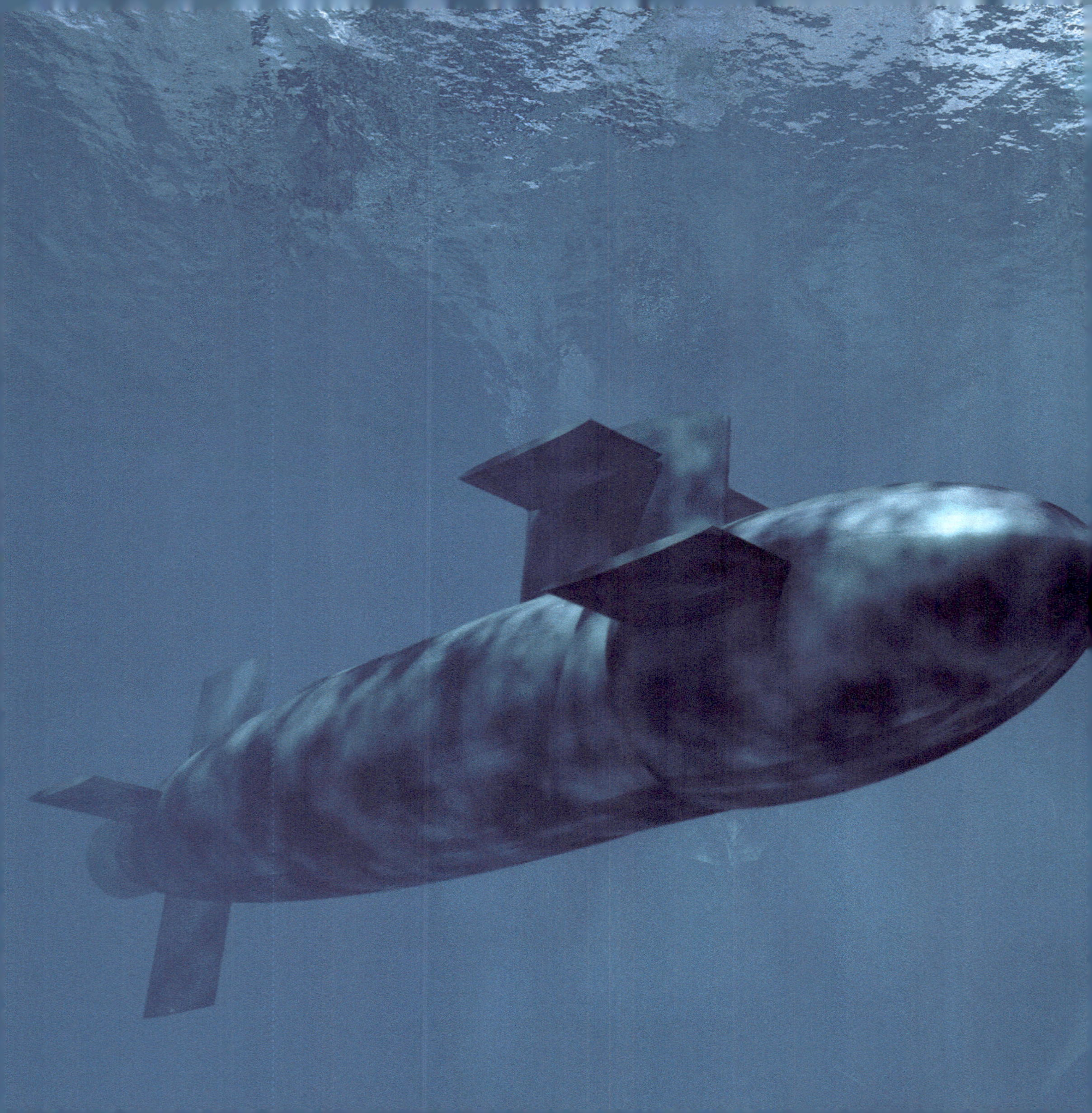

Many other adventurers managed to get to the North Pole by airplane over the next decades, and in 1958 a United States submarine was able to travel to the North Pole and surface there.

But it was not until 1986 that anybody was able to walk to the North Pole.

In that year, explorer Will Steger became the first person to make it to the North Pole over land and without airdrops of supplies, and he only managed it after several tries.

There have been many other polar expeditions, some for scientific research and others to set records. For example, Shinji Kazama of Japan in 1987 was the first person to ride a motorcycle to the North Pole!

EXPEDITIONERS AT NORTH POLE

THOMAS H. NAST

SANTA AND THE NORTH POLE

The idea that Santa Claus has his headquarters at the North Pole became popular after an artist, Thomas Nast, published a series of drawings of Santa's workshop in 1879. This seized the imagination of people in many nations.

Canada, the United States, and many other countries maintain postal addresses so people can write to Santa Claus, and at Christmas time each year the North American Air Defense system (NORAD) tracks the progress of Santa's sleigh as his reindeer pull it south on the way to bring presents to every home.

A BOY WRITING A CHRISTMAS LETTER TO SANTA CLAUS

SUFI DANCER

This new tradition connects with ancient beliefs about the far north being the home of gods or supernatural beings. In Iran, for example, Sufi tradition holds that the "north beyond the north" is a mystical place of great spiritual strength.

One of the problems with Santa's workshop being at the North Pole is that there is no land to build it on. Unless it is a floating workshop, it must be hidden away elsewhere, among the mountains of Canada, Norway, Russia, or another Arctic country.

Alaska
(U.S.)
ANADA
Wrangel
Island
New
Siberian
Islands
Banks
Island
Victoria
Island
Queen Elizabeth Islands
RUSSIA
Severnaya
Zemlya
North
Pole
Ellesmere Isl.
Franz Josef
Land
Baffin
Island
Novaya
Zemlya
Svalbard
(NORWAY)
Greenland
(DENMARK)
Jan Mayen
(NORWAY)
ICELAND
SWEDEN
NORWAY

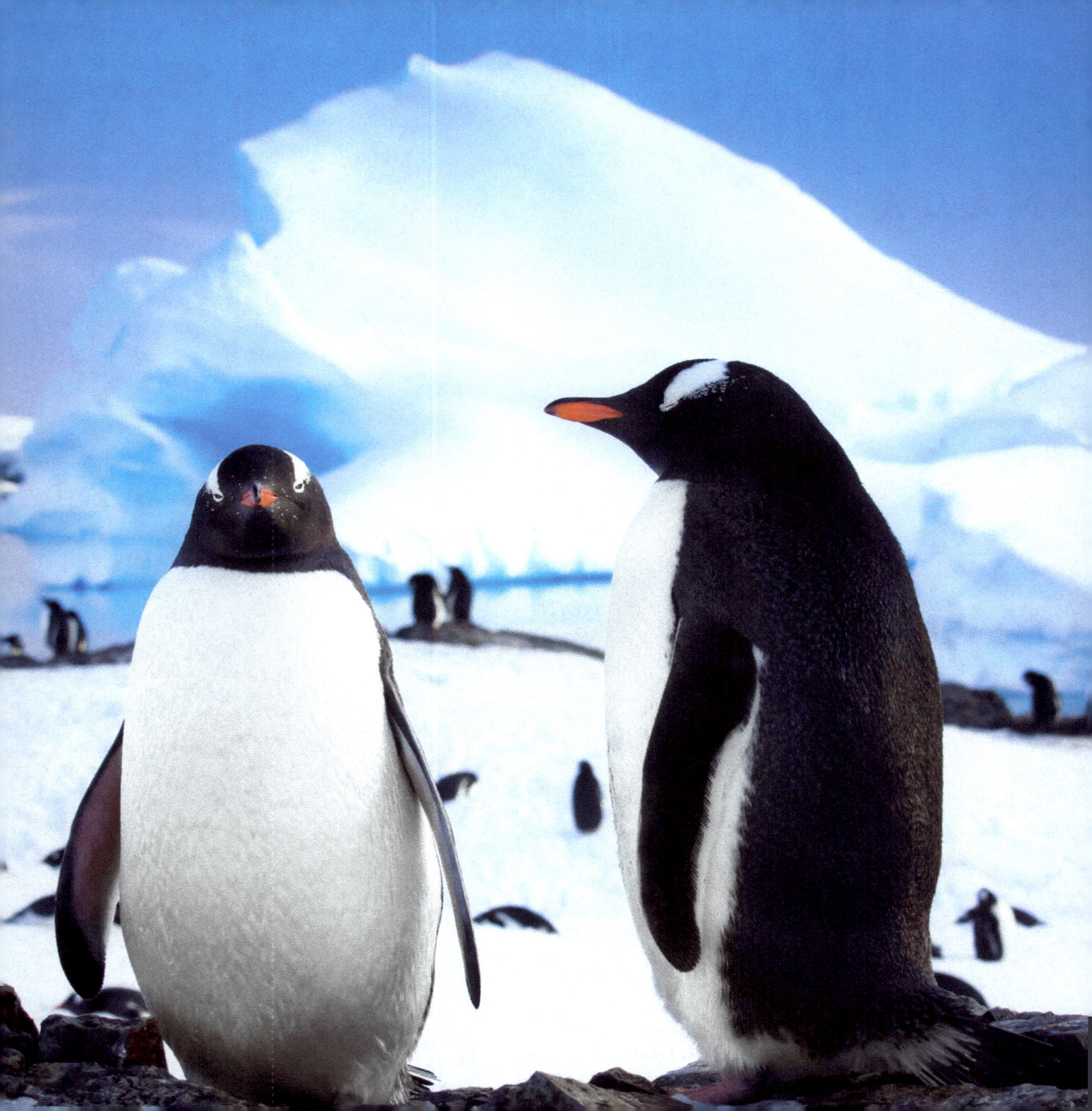

THEN WHO LIVES AT THE POLE?

If Santa Claus doesn't live at the North Pole, then who does? Actually, almost no animals live at the Pole. There is little or nothing to eat there, and any animals seen at the pole would be passing through as they hunt or travel for other reasons.

A 2006 polar expedition reported seeing a polar bear about a mile from the North Pole, but polar bears almost never travel further north than 82 degrees north latitude. There is simply not enough for them to eat closer to the Pole.

POLAR BEAR MOTHER WITH TWO CUBS ON THE ICE

ARCTIC FOX

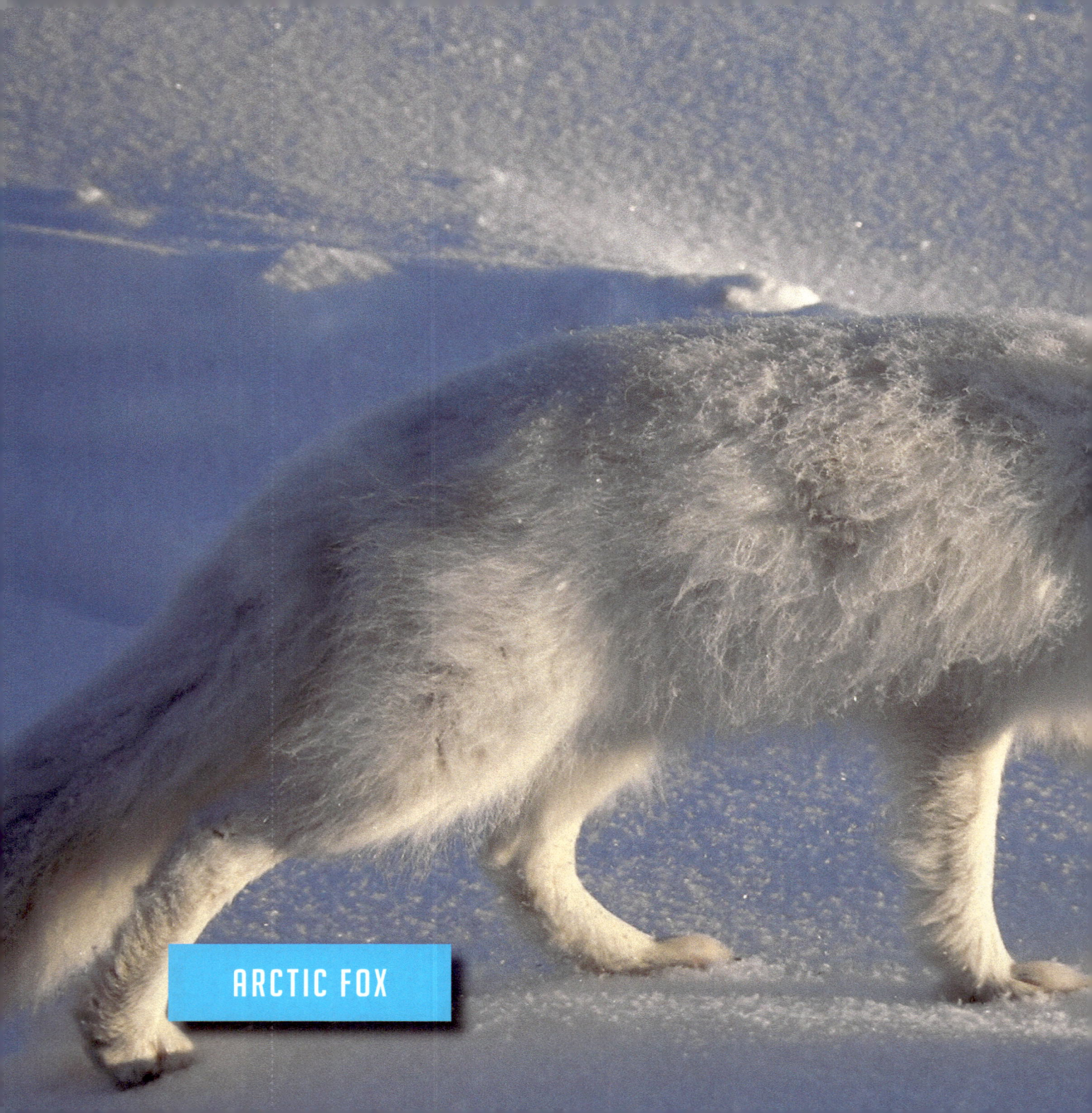

Ringed seals and arctic foxes are occasional polar visitors, but they are not permanent residents.

Even seals would find it tough to live at the North Pole, as the Arctic Ocean is not home to many species of fish. There are some species of shrimp and crab that make a living in the mud at the bottom of the Arctic Ocean, but it must be a lonely life!

RINGED SEAL

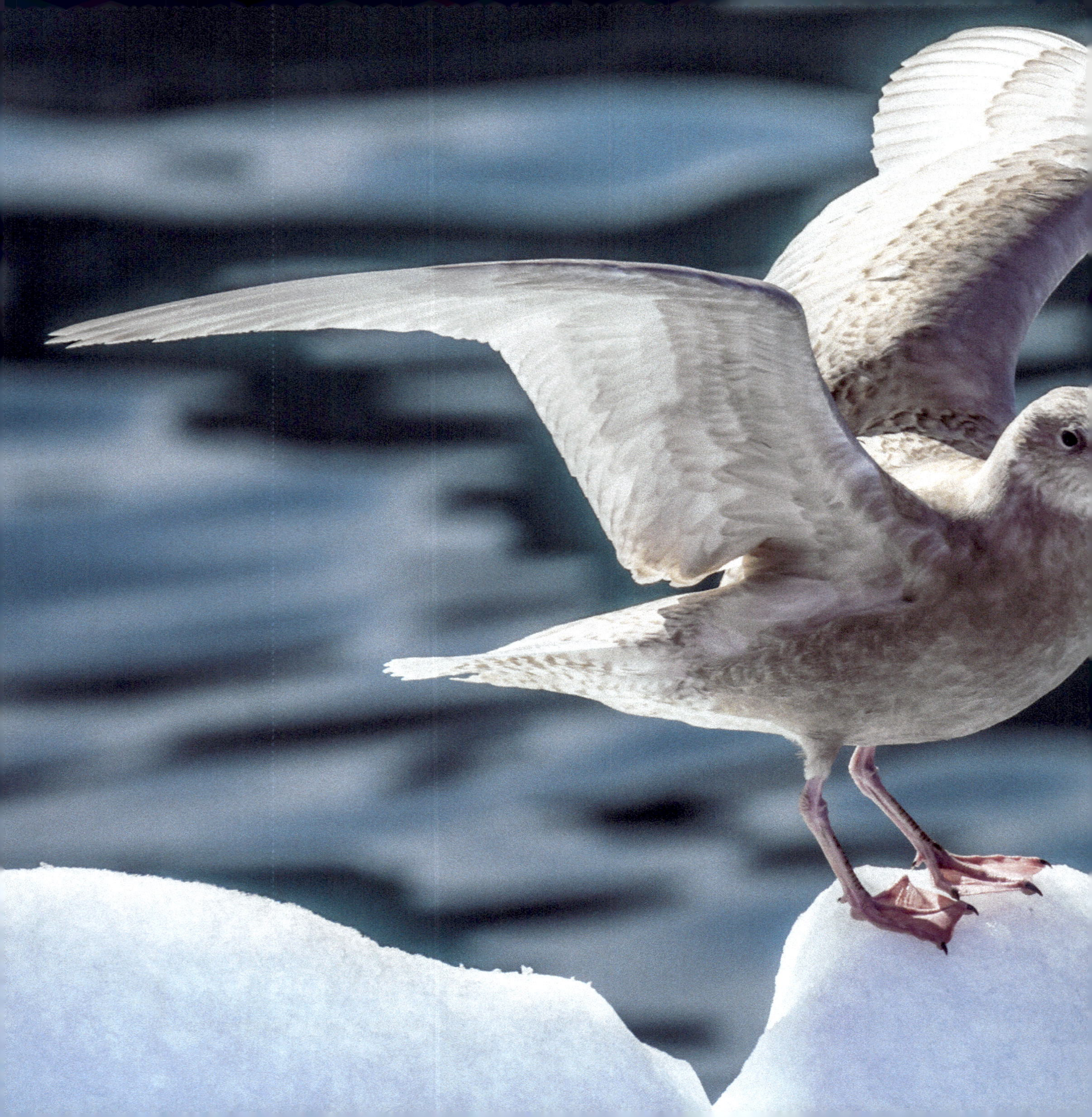

Birds fly over and near the North Pole, including snow buntings, northern fulmars, and other hardy birds.

FULMAR ON AN ICEBERG

However, some of them may have been following the ships of the scientists who saw them; it is hard to say if they would have chosen to go to the North Pole if there was not a chance of eating food scraps from a ship.

SNOW BUNTING

NORTH POLE

POLE TO POLE

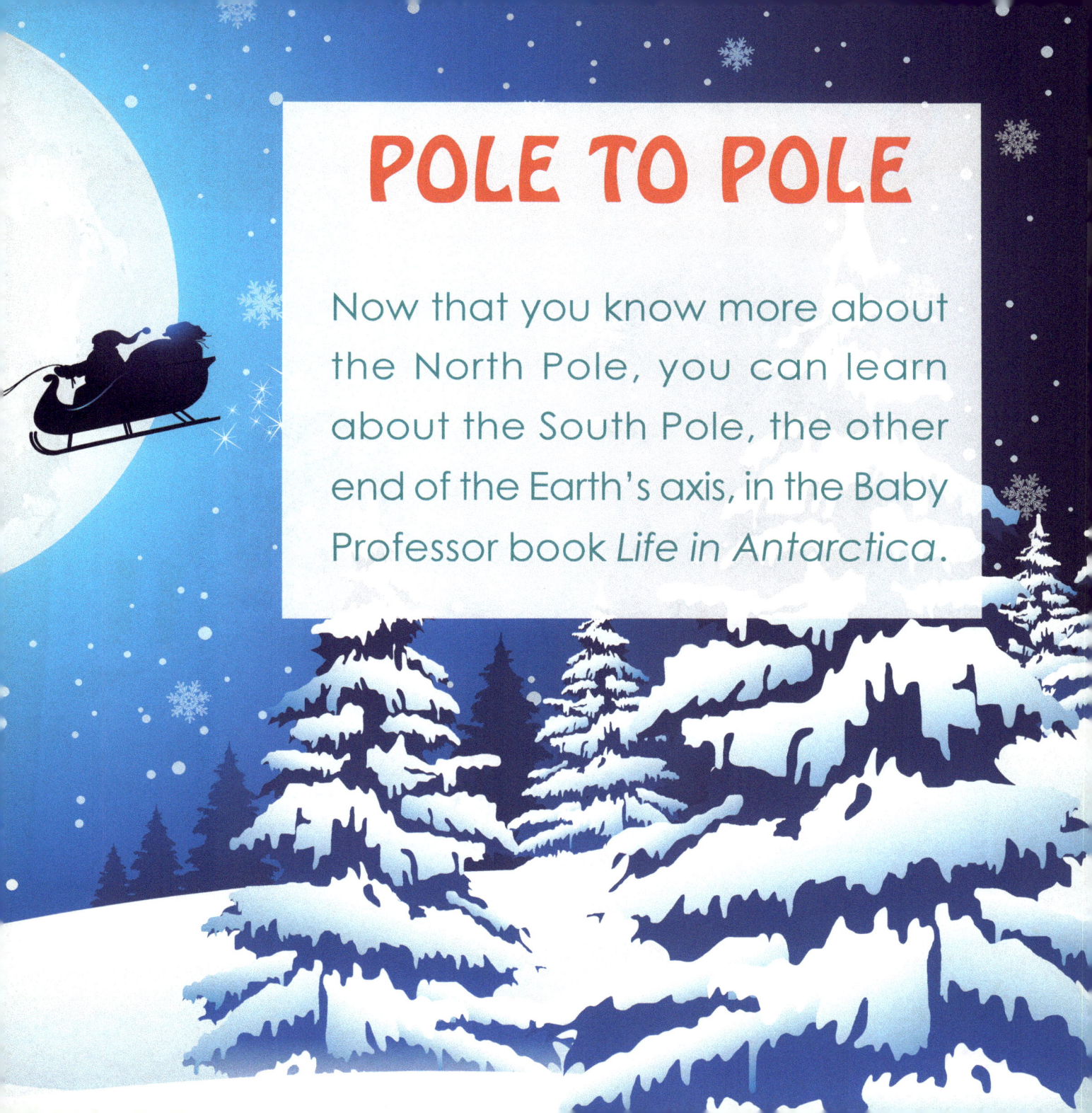

Now that you know more about the North Pole, you can learn about the South Pole, the other end of the Earth's axis, in the Baby Professor book *Life in Antarctica*.

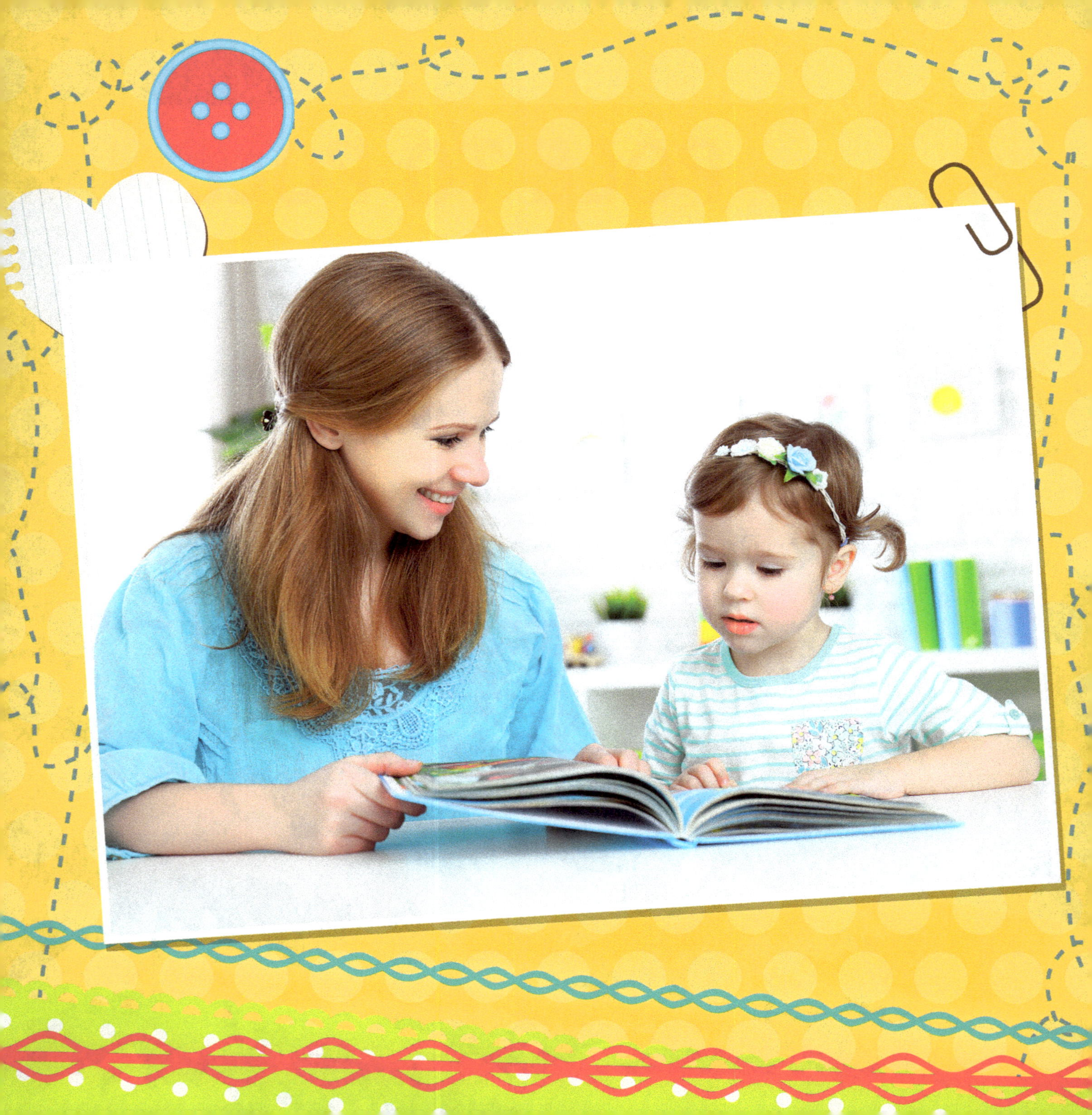

Visit

BABY PROFESSOR
EDUCATION KIDS

www.BabyProfessorBooks.com

to download Free Baby Professor eBooks
and view our catalog of new and exciting
Children's Books

Milton Keynes UK
Ingram Content Group UK Ltd.
UKHW051124030924
447802UK00003B/51

9 798869 417725